This page is intentionaly left blank.

Becoming

Sarah Rewega

© 2021 Ingramspark

All rights reserved. No part of this publication may be reproduced, stored in a retrieval system or transmited in any form or by any means, electronic, mechanical, photocopying, recording or otherwise without the prior permision of the publisher or in accordance with the provisions of the Copyright, Designs and Patents Act 1988 or under the terms of any licence permitting limited copying issued by the Copyright Licensing Angency.

Cover Design: Sarah Rewega

ISBN: 9781777924409

Printed in USA

To my roommate Waed,

who encouraged, supported

and pushed me to

do this project, and

to my parents who relentlessly

supported and believed in me,

this book is for you.

Finally: to all the women fighting battles,

no matter what they may be, may

you conquer—may you **become.**

Contents

Becoming 6

Became 24

Becoming

noun

PHILOSOPHY

1. the process of coming to be *something* or of passing into a state.

"a series of poem sketches in a state of becoming"

"Becoming"

is

a loaded term.

Like a bullet,

it arrives at your doorstep

when you least expect it.

The dark forest
Overwhelms me
So much so
That it becomes me
And yet,
The dark lustful trees welcome me

They remind me that loneliness is consuming
And getting lost in such hypnotic places

Can be free
                ing

Until you wake up.

It's not about the sad emerald green haze in the distance

falling off the trees in the spot where we used to sit watching the sunset

and it's not about the sorrowing emerald green accents in the distance

peeking out of the forest,

where we used to go when we wanted to be wild and free

It's about the way the water wraps its way around me when I want to drown

It keeps me afloat.

The river flowed through the course as it should on Sunday November fourteenth.

It was particularly cold that day.

I remember how the body of water looked contrasted against the crimson sky and the way that the willow tree wept below the gulf

But most of all I remember the feeling I felt when the pace of the river began, and my heart began to race alongside

Mirroring each wave, slowly and softly

My gaze met the rock and I swear it smiled back at me.

The river was particularly cold that day.

But November 15th never came.

It's the wretchedly wretched heart wrenching gutting feeling I get when I investigate the future

It's the clear day easy listening

Soft crystals and light breezy snow floating in the air

When I pretend it doesn't exist.

It contrasts against the dark crimson nights on first street where I feel unsafe in my life.

Decisions can be a doubled surface

Troubled and complicated

Relieving and appeasing

On one hand, it can be silky smooth, crystalline lightly breezy

And on the other, it can be daunting and hellish

And if I had to choose

I wouldn't.

I feel this unease of fire burn deep within me

Manifesting its way into my soul

Finding its way in every crack and crevice of my

mind and body

These cracks,

They are evidence of my wounds—

Complications, unease, un-comfort, general

sadness?

"No",

They say.

Trauma,

That's what we call it here.

when she spoke to me that day

I knew it wasn't really her speaking to me like that

But the parts of her that weren't yet healed.

I told you to stop taking up so much space

He said.

I crumbled and I fumbled until I fell to the ground
Certain I couldn't shrink anymore
Shrinking for you was the worst thing I've ever done

And believe me
I've done stupid things

I told myself I would no longer shrink
And treat my body
Like a disposable garbage bag
Flying away in the wind
And so I sit on the brown couch,

I stare at the photo.

Remembering the one time where I tried to move
And you told me to take less space
To suit your needs

Like a puppet.

I refuse to be a mindless, senseless doll
For someone that can't define the word patriarchy
Misogyny is your middle name after all,

Isn't it?

Weeping willowed eyes

And hollowed dry mouths

Crinkle together

Charging toward the unknown.

Here, we welcome what is unknown.

Scents of sage and parsley consume the room
I tried my favourite dress on last night
The one that reminds me of u
I can't seem to forget what it was like
When I was happy
When waking up wasn't a struggle
And questions didn't consume my day

Because I lost myself so quick so deeply in those scents of parsley.
I sit there and think
Who would I be without you?
If I hadn't met this version of myself,
I throw away the parsley and sage and I say,

"Well, for one, I'd be free of parsley and sage"

In the light breeze and dark turning trees, I see her

Visions of her embedded in the shaded accents of

red and yellow

A soft and gentle version of her arrives on my door

step
A version of who she used to be

A version of who she was

And in the echoes of the light breeze
I hear her voice,

The way she laughed in harmony,

Until she could no longer breathe

I hear the voice of someone who appeared green

Until she turned into the crippling shades of yellow and red,

In the middle of fall.

I remember kissing the Peter Pan DVD at the age of 6 thinking to myself how easy life would be

If only Peter Pan had noticed me

He was the boy that never wanted to be found

And I was the girl who so desperately wanted to be.

The soft tropical beats begin to consume every spec of space in the room

Until there is nothing left,

Endless music and trembling thoughts drown out the sounds, one beat falling at a time

Like dominoes.

But our existence is not as simple as a game of

dominoes

Nor is it as beautiful as the tropical beats in the room next door

So I walk toward the music

And I choose to ignore

That life isn't a simple game of dominoes—

For a few minutes longer.

the warm summer breeze caressed me so deeply my bones shook on that Sunday evening

But nothing could shake the feeling of uncertainty

Not even the breeze could heal the eminent questions lingering from my fingertips all the way to my tongue

The questions vibrate through me but nothing can stop the feeling of being absent from yourself

My bones rattle.

Because I know that not even the breeze would help me find myself this time.

I once knew a man
Who only saw
The black and white
In me
He consumed my thoughts
Back in 2015

One summer night,
He gazed at me
titling his head
With his piercing eyes
And said
"You're my monochromic muse"
White butterflies fluttered around in my stomach,
And then I turned away
Blushing shades of black,
Realizing I was becoming
The very thing
I never wanted to become...

A colorless c a r c a s s.

Part 2:
she became

Became

Instransitive verb

PHILOSOPHY

1.To come into existence

Inhale
Like a field of wildflowers
You were my eden—

Until I realized you are the place where flowers go to die.

Without you,
I am a daisy, illuminating from grace
Though delicately sensitive
I flourish from this freedom.
Learning to live without you
Is a breath of fresh air.

Exhale
You were my eden,

But now I am a wildflower.
In my own garden of opportunity.

It poured late that night
Until the sun rose
And swept away the grievances of the day.

She wondered around in the forest,
wondering when it would stop,
The loud drops flicker on the palm trees.

She didn't know it would happen so soon
But when the sun came up he knew
That her search was complete
The rain had stopped.

It found her first.

It found her first like the sun found the rain
Different, I suppose.

But still wonderful.

The essence of sage caresses my mind,
Bringing me back to a time where they told me

*"Dear,
Stay calm
And stay wild
But don't be too much
Or too little"*

The smell of sea salt and beach sand remains lingering on my body
Just like these voices do
Passive, but constant
Embedding themselves within me

And while this place may linger on in my mind until the day I die

I will always remember the day where I escaped
The day I found the person I am supposed to be
Not the person they told me to be.

Quaint, multi-faceted places
Looming with green tropical trees
Blissful scents and cherished memories

A scarce look is all it takes to see it
The blooming flowers age in front of me
Gracefully and elegantly

They speak to me one morning
A faint echo in my ear
They tell me
That I too
Am blooming
And becoming the person I have always wanted to be

They say,

"That girl is powerful
The one who sought freedom
Moves mountains and rivers
With her mind
That is the one that knows her worth."

He looks at me and whispers; "I love you"
Like a cup of warm tea—
Comforting and enticing.
I embellish myself within you.

Then winter came.
Sufferable frosty frigid and frozen.
He's decided he doesn't love me anymore.
Misery, sufferance, I am frosty frigid and paralyzed—
I am frozen.

Then spring came.
I told myself that I'll be okay.

But most importantly,
I reminded myself that,

*"Like all of the beautiful flowers that bloom in the spring despite the heavy winters,
I will bloom.
I will bloom too"*

Thank you
For showing me

That after being caged in the deepest and darkest
places of your mind

There is light within me.

Like the weeping willowed trees
Make statements with their beauty
We make statements with our voices

When the lightening stops, and the sky begins to clear

I sit there and drink my peach mango tea

The sweet bitter taste sets me into a trance

Words seeping slowly from the tea bag

Wild in taste
Wild in thought

The mango tea spells it out
With intricate yet fluid words
They tell me one thing:
They tell me it's you.
They tell me it's your time.

You.
My daily dose of sunshine-like peach mango tea,

"My wandering yellow sun"
She says.

Wander until you find what you're looking for.

It felt like dark green trees
Soft rain and Bon Iver
Ivory skin silhouetted and dark yellow eyes

Don't let it fool you this time
She said,
As she grew trees around her with her mind.

Her mind,
It felt like a dark green forest
Complicated and dusky

The sound of the subtle rain and the paper kites
Mimic her ambiance

And in loud wind bustling against the trees, she knew

She knew everything would be alright.

It would always be alright.

And when I get there,

These unchartered waters will no longer be yours

But a faint memory

Of what was.

Remember me

I am the girl that swam away
Refusing to drown.

Remember me.

I am that girl that found freedom

In her own body of water.

"Became"
is
a term that signals transition.

Like a bullet,
it arrives at your doorstep.
But this time it's different...

You know it's coming.

Became.

She *came* into existence.

www.ingramcontent.com/pod-product-compliance
Lightning Source LLC
Chambersburg PA
CBHW072210100526
44589CB00015B/2462